Stevie Wonder

Sunshine In The Shadow

Stevie Wonder

Sunshine In The Shadow

By Linda Jacobs

EMC CORPORATION
ST. PAUL, MINNESOTA

Library of Congress Cataloging in Publication Data

Jacobs, Linda.
   Stevie Wonder: sunshine in the shadow.
   (Men behind the bright lights)
   SUMMARY: A biography tracing the rise to stardom of a black musician who was blind from birth.
   1. Wonder, Stevie — Juvenile literature.
[1. Wonder, Stevie. 2. Musicians. 3. Afro-Americans — Biography] I. Title.
ML3930.W65J3 784'.092'4 [B] [92] 75-33012
ISBN 0-88436-257-4
ISBN 0-88436-258-2 pbk.

Copyright 1976 by EMC Corporation.
All rights reserved. Published 1976.

No part of this publication can be reproduced, stored in a retrieval system, or transmitted in any form or by any means; electronic, mechanical, photocopying, recording, or otherwise, without the permission of the publisher.

Published by EMC Corporation
180 East Sixth Street
St. Paul, Minnesota 55101
Printed in the United States of America
0 9 8 7 6 5 4 3 2

MEN BEHIND THE BRIGHT LIGHTS

ELTON JOHN • REGINALD DWIGHT & CO.
JIM CROCE • THE FEELING LIVES ON
STEVIE WONDER • SUNSHINE IN THE SHADOW
JOHN DENVER • A NATURAL HIGH

WOMEN BEHIND THE BRIGHT LIGHTS

OLIVIA NEWTON-JOHN • SUNSHINE SUPERGIRL
VALERIE HARPER • THE UNFORGETTABLE SNOWFLAKE
ROBERTA FLACK • SOUND OF VELVET MELTING
CHER • SIMPLY CHER

Nothing was going right.

Stagehands tripped over each other trying to fix a sound system that refused to work right. Several instruments hadn't arrived yet. Two stage lights weren't working and three musicians felt like they were coming down with the flu. And a major concert was only minutes away.

In the midst of all the confusion, Stevie Wonder sat in his dressing room, surrounded by friends, co-workers, and his fiancée, Yolanda.

"Stevie, it's just not coming together," someone said.

"It will, it will," Stevie said with a laugh. Then he went back to the new tune he was working out on the Moog Synthesizer. In the midst of all the confusion he cracked an

A view from the stage crowded with sound equipment, piano (center), and Moog Synthesizer (left). A sell-out crowd packed the Forum in Los Angeles in 1974 for a Stevie Wonder concert.

occasional joke, answered countless questions, let Yolanda pick out his Afro, and still managed to work on a new song.

"Every concert is like this. I don't know how he does it," a friend said.

Stevie shrugged and tried a couple more chord changes. Then it was time. By some miracle, the musical instruments had arrived. The lights and sound system had been fixed. Stevie's backup musicians had forgotten all about flu as they stood in front of an audience of thousands and started the opening music.

"It's time to go," said Stevie's

The many faces of the Wonder man, spreading his special sunshine.

brother, Calvin. Yolanda took a final jab at Stevie's hair, then put down the pick. Stevie stood up and stretched.

"Where are my dark glasses?" he blurted suddenly. His dressing room exploded into a flurry of activity. Calvin checked the bathroom. Yolanda plowed through heaps of things on the dresser. Someone else pulled cushions off the couch. Outside, they could hear the music building. Stevie had only seconds to make his entrance.

"Here they are," Yolanda yelled, retrieving them from a dresser drawer. Stevie grabbed the glasses and jammed them onto his face. He held onto Calvin's arm as the two of them made a dash for the stage. Stevie made his entrance at exactly the right moment.

Backstage, everyone collapsed with sighs of relief. Onstage, under the glaring lights he could not see, Stevie began once again to prove why Motown Records changed his last name to "Wonder."

His head rolled with the music. His voice reached out to those thousands of people as if he was singing to each one, individually.

The audience swayed with him, felt with him. They didn't know about the pandemonium backstage. They wouldn't have cared, anyway. What mattered was the Wonder man with his mellow voice, his musical genius, his special sunshine.

"He really is a wonder," someone in the audience whispered.

And he is. But getting it that way — bringing the sunshine out of the shadow — wasn't an easy task.

When Steveland Judkins Morris was born, on May 13, 1950, the doctors shook their heads and told Lula Mae Morris that her son was born blind and likely would always be that way. She broke into tears.

Blind and black and poor — what kind of a life could this new infant have? In her wildest dreams, Mrs. Morris could never

have imagined that her new baby would become a rich and famous musician called Stevie Wonder. At the time, all she could do was pray — and worry.

Stevie himself didn't worry at all. Life was too full. He was reared among church-going people whose faith helped them bear the poverty. Music was always part of his life. He would listen to blues singer B.B. King and pound spoons or forks on any surface that faintly resembled a drum.

He even ran and played with sighted children. "I didn't realize I was blind until I was about four," he says. That might sound strange. To a small child just learning about the world, it wasn't strange at all. Stevie heard and smelled and touched. As far as he knew, that was all anyone could do. That was life.

He found out that he lacked something others took for granted when he came in from a backyard romp with dog manure all over his shoes and tracked it on his mother's clean floor.

"Stevie," she wailed, and whacked him once in sheer frustration.

"But Ma," Stevie protested, "how was I supposed to know it

was there?"

His mother sighed and hugged him.

"You can't . . . but you shouldn't be running and jumping around like you did know."

It suddenly hit Stevie that his mother would have known where to step and where not to step. Slowly, it all came together — the way his mother worried about him more than she did about the other children. The way everyone else knew what was on their plates at dinner while he had to be told. He was different.

"Even then, it didn't really bother me," Stevie says. Stevie payed so little attention to his blindness that he regularly frightened his mother half out of her wits.

The whack he got for tracking up the floor wasn't his last spanking. He got one the time he shinnied up a tree to steal apples. He got one the time he jumped from the roof of one shed to another, with only a friend's voice to guide him to his target. His mother fussed and fumed and lectured, but secretly she was almost pleased with Stevie's hijinks.

He was a normal kid, getting into trouble for normal pranks. Blindness wasn't holding him back. In fact, it began to look like nothing could hold him back, especially with his music.

When his mother got tired of her tables being used for drums, she bought him a toy set. He played so hard that he had actually worn the toy out within a few weeks. Other toy sets followed; then an uncle added a toy harmonica, and Stevie learned to play it so quickly that everyone was amazed.

Not all of Stevie's life was as happy as the time he spent with

Stevie and his mother, Mrs. Lula Hardaway at Stevie's birthday party. Singer Bill Withers is on the right.

music. His father had never been much of a family man. One day he simply took off.

Lula Mae Morris moved herself and her children to Detroit, Michigan. For Stevie, that move was quite a blow. He missed his friends and his home church. He missed the feeling of space he'd had in his hometown of Saginaw.

In Detroit, he felt crowded and poorer than ever. He also became conscious of being black. He went to a mostly-white school and began to notice differences between himself and the other students. They thought different thoughts, practiced their religions in different ways. They even listened to different music.

Stevie used to sit on the school bus with his transistor radio turned low so he could listen to B.B. King without the others knowing. The blues was black music — music that set Stevie apart frim his white schoolmates.

Stevie kept hiding his black

Stevie was only thirteen when he went to Paris to appear at the Olympia Music Hall with a young British star Louise Cordet. The newspapers called him Little Stevie Wonder and said he was "so talented he might become a new Ray Charles."

music, but homesickness didn't last for long. Stevie found a new church and began to sing in the choir. He made new friends. He even got a new step-father when his mother remarried. Best of all, he got a set of real drums at a Lions Club party for blind children and a piano from a neighbor who was moving away.

Stevie taught himself to play piano as quickly as he had once learned the harmonica. With friends, he began playing rock and roll music. They held jam sessions on the front porch of Stevie's apartment building, drawing crowds of neighbors to watch and listen and clap time to the beat.

"I loved that beat," Stevie says. He not only loved the beat, he was very good at making it. His talent was so big, so real, that someone just had to come along and spot it.

Someone did. Ronnie White, of The Miracles singing group, was a cousin of Stevie's playmate, John Glover. Ronnie heard Stevie and promptly took him down to his recording company, Motown Records.

Always eager to perform, Stevie strikes up an impromptu jam session with friends at his birthday party.

"Give him an audition," Ronnie said. They did. All the top people at Motown got together to hear a little blind boy who wasn't even ten years old yet. At first, they were being nice. Poor kid. They didn't want to hurt his feelings.

Then they heard Stevie sing and play, and nobody said "poor kid" anymore. They were too busy congratulating themselves on finding a youngster who could be the musical talent of the decade.

Stevie started going to Motown's offices every day after school. He hung around and listened to everybody else's music and grabbed every chance to play some of his own. Everyone there called him "Little Stevie."

"He'd play anything he could get his hands on," says Clarence Paul, the man who became Stevie's musical conductor.

Today, everyone at Motown has grown used to Stevie's talent. At the time, they could barely believe what they saw and heard. Never had any of them seen such pure natural ability in a young child.

"He's a wonder boy," Clarence said one day, as he watched little Stevie dart from one instrument to another, playing

each one with ease.

"Wonder," somebody said. "Little Stevie Wonder."

Clarence's eyes started to glow. "That's it," he said, in a voice that was filled with quiet discovery. "That's what we'll call him on his records."

The name stuck and Stevie Morris became Little Stevie Wonder. He had his first hit when he was twelve years old. It was called "Fingertips" and it was a smash, topping charts all over the country.

Little Stevie Wonder was on his way. He had the music he loved and more money than his family had ever seen. "It was great," Stevie says. "Half the time, I couldn't believe it was all for real."

Clarence Paul and other people who worked at Motown felt a great responsibility for such a young and talented boy. They had to manage his time so that he could be a normal kid as well as a star. They had to manage his money and see that he received a good education. Most of all, they had to deal with a musical giant in the body of a little boy.

"Sometimes we had to pull him off the stage at concerts," Clarence says. Stevie loved performing so much that he would keep going as long as the audiences and the Motown people would let him. When Clarence insisted, "this has to be the last number," Stevie would sulk like a kid who has just been told that he can't play until his homework is done.

For Stevie, the problems

came with balancing school work and performing. The school problem was solved for Stevie when his parents and Motown records took him out of public schools. He went to the Michigan School for the Blind and had a private tutor who went with him on tour.

Stevie solved another problem all by himself. It all started one day when he was having a jam session with some of the neighborhood kids, a lady from his church came by.

"How can you play that worldly music? Stevie, I'm ashamed of you — a boy who sings in the choir!"

"But he's a star," chirped one of Stevie's playmates. "He makes records." Stevie winced. He could hear the woman's sharp gasp. He knew there would be trouble — and he was right. The next week, the choir director informed him that it wouldn't be proper for a boy who was so involved with worldly music to continue singing in the choir.

Backstage Stevie waits with friends Dick Griffey, his promoter, and Chris Jonz his manager. Yolanda is behind Stevie.

"But I got as much faith as anybody," Stevie protested. "Besides, I sing good." Stevie could feel the disapproval, hear the sigh. He didn't say any more. He just turned and walked away. He went home and cried, but he couldn't bring himself to feel that he was doing wrong. He thought of B.B. King and the soul songs he had always loved. How could that music — any music be bad?

Through music, Stevie could reach others, share the faith that conquered poverty and blindness.

In 1967, before his accident, before his Innervisions *album, before Syreeta, Stevie presented quite a different image from today. He was seventeen when this picture was taken.*

Surely God could understand that — even if the church didn't.

As Stevie thought about all those things, something special happened inside him. Music had always been his joy, but he had simply drifted into his professional career. It seemed like a happy accident. Standing up to the choir director had made him realize that his career was going to be more than a fluke that would last for a few records. It was going to be his life.

With that decision, Stevie settled down to work. He practiced hard and repeated recording sessions over and over, until they were just right.

His concerts were still studies in disorganization. Each one looked like it would fall through before Stevie ever got onstage. Each one came off perfectly, in spite of the problems. One thing did change, though. Stevie no longer kept going until Clarence had to pull him off the stage. That wasn't the professional thing to do.

Above all, Stevie was a real professional. He recorded hit after hit — songs like "Uptight," and "My Cherie Amour." As he met more people through his work, something else began happening to him. He started taking new pride in being black.

He couldn't see the color of his own skin or anybody else's. But he could hear the pain and dignity of black music, taste the difference between soul food and other dishes. He looked back on the little boy who hid his B.B. King music. That was dumb, he told himself.

With that final acceptance of himself, Stevie had it all together. He knew where he wanted to go in life — now he knew who he was. More than ever, he seemed like an adult genius in a child's body.

Stevie and Syreeta announced their engagement in June, 1970.

Then even the body changed.

By the time he was eighteen, he topped six feet and the "Little" in front of his name sounded ridiculous.

"We've got to drop it," Clarence said.

"Yes," Stevie said, "I guess we do." He didn't feel little anymore. He felt grown and strong and ready to fly.

And he did fly — personally as well as professionally. In 1970 he married Syreeta Wright. She was a secretary at Motown and a talented songwriter and singer in her own right. Together, Stevie and Syreeta wrote "Love Having You Around," and other tender and gentle songs.

To Stevie, Syreeta was the miracle of the age. It was wonderful having someone special to share his life, his hopes. She seemed to understand his religious faith, his love of music. She respected him for his pride and for conquering his blindness.

"Syreeta made me feel like expanding," Stevie says. Stevie's expansion took him in strange new musical directions. He began to resent the way Motown supervised his every move. They managed his money, his recording time, his concert schedule. Worse, they had complete control over the songs he wrote and performed. His music had to fit the Motown formula or it just wouldn't be accepted.

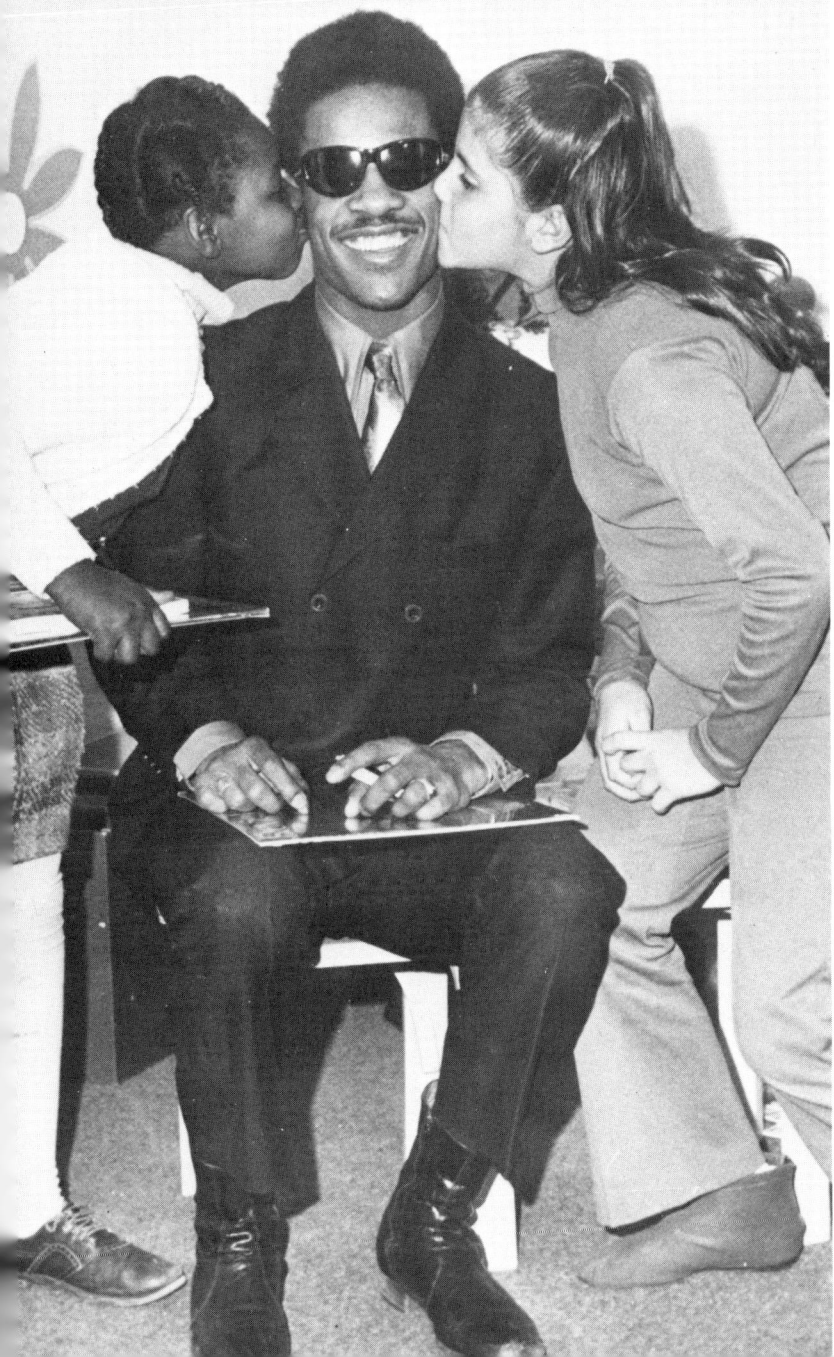

Stevie got thank you kisses from two young admirers the day he visited the Eye Institute in New York and presented his albums to the young patients there. He was awarded the Fight for Sight Show Business Inspiration Award of 1969.

"I want to try new things," Stevie said, but nobody listened. They patted him on the back and said that he already had a winning formula. Stick with it.

But he couldn't. When his contract came up for renewal, he refused to sign unless he had artistic freedom.

"You can't do this, Stevie . . . you just can't," everyone at Motown said.

Stevie ached inside. These

Mrs. Richard Nixon, the President's wife, thanked Stevie for attending the "Summer in the Park" program in Washington, D.C. Stevie had helped calm the crowd after someone booed Mrs. Nixon. The man in the center is the Mayor of Washington.

were his friends. Maybe they were right — maybe he was being disloyal. He prayed a lot and thought a lot. He remembered the time, years before, when he had been kicked out of the church choir. He had done what he felt was right then. He had to do it now.

"I've got to have a new contract," he said, and the firmness in his voice left no doubt that he meant what he said.

Stevie got his contract with full artistic freedom — and with more money than he'd ever dreamed of. He started making new and exciting albums like *Talking Book* and *Innervisions*.

He felt good about the music, but he was nervous. What if the public didn't like his musical experiments. What if he really was wrong? To add to his worries, he and Syreeta had begun to have problems. His professional life and personal life were beginning to clash in a way they'd never done before.

Stevie's first worry dissolved

Stevie appeared at an outdoor concert for the Watts Summer Fest in Los Angeles in 1974, not long after he recovered from his accident.

in a flurry of public acceptance and critical praise. He had been right! Everybody at Motown gladly admitted that. They even made plans to let their other artists be more involved in selecting their own music.

"It was beautiful," Stevie says.

But there was still the problems with Syreeta. She and Stevie still liked each other, still worked well together, but marriage was a special strain. They were

Stevie won four Grammy awards again in 1975, including Best Album of the Year. Here he poses with Bette Midler who presented the award.

In 1974 Stevie was nominated for more Grammy awards than anyone ever in the recording industry. He won four.

seriously wondering if they could make it together when a tragedy temporarily wiped out the whole question.

On August 6, 1973, Stevie was riding in a car outside of Winston-Salem, North Carolina. In a freak accident, the car hit a lumber truck. One log smashed through the windshield and jammed against Stevie's skull.

After all the sirens and emergency aid and police investigation, the man who had once been Little Stevie, the Wonder boy, lay in a hospital room, deep in a coma. The coma lasted for nearly a week, while doctors fought to save his life.

"We don't even know when he'll be out of danger," the doctors said. Everyone waited and prayed. Suddenly it didn't matter that Stevie was a musical genius or that he was black and proud or even that he had conquered

blindness and poverty. All he had left was his faith and strong will.

That turned out to be enough.

Stevie's good friend Ira Tucker found that out when he went into the hospital room. At first, he sat quietly, watching Stevie's still and battered body. When he started to talk, Stevie didn't move.

Ira left the room with tears in his eyes. Later he came back and something made him decide to sing. He took Stevie's limp hand into his own and leaned close. In his loudest voice, Ira began to sing one of Stevie's songs, "Higher Ground."

Ira sang with tears in his eyes and a lump in his throat. Then he felt something — Stevie's hand started to move. His fingers drummed softly — in perfect time to the music!

"He's gonna make it," Ira crowed.

And Stevie did make it. He fought back from the shadow of death as he had once fought out from the shadow of blindness. He went on to give more performances, make more hit records.

He still had to face the sadness of the final breakup of his marriage to Syreeta. "We just couldn't get it back together," he says.

At first, Stevie felt lost and frightened. There was an empty hole in his life. Then he met Yolanda and he found that the love he held inside him was far from spent.

Stevie and Yolanda were greeted by Mayor Bradley after a special appearance at Los Angeles City Hall.

A group of eager school children reach out to touch Stevie — the star, the Wonder man.

Today, Stevie's world is filled with Yolanda, his friends and his family. It's crowded with recording sessions and those hopelessly disorganized concerts that somehow always turn out in the end.

At twenty-five, Stevie has faith and fame, wealth and love. He understands and accepts himself — a man who has conquered his own darkness and can bring sunshine to the shadow of other lives.

PHOTO CREDITS

Motown Records: 11, 34
Bruce Talamon: 6-7, 8, 12, 14, 18, 20, 23, 32, 33, 36, 39
United Press International Photos: 24, 27, 30, 34 (top)
Wide World Photos: 17, 28, 29, 35